Adam's New Soccer Team

by Will Lee
Illustrated by Gary Torrisi

PEARSON

Glenview, Illinois • Boston, Massachusetts • Chandler, Arizona
Upper Saddle River, New Jersey

It was the first day of soccer practice.
Adam did not know anyone.
He missed his old team.
Adam wanted to play with his friends.

"Welcome to your new team,"
said Coach. "Let's practice."
Adam smiled at Chuck and Lara.
They were on the team too.

The team passed the ball.
They kicked the ball to each other.
They worked together.

It was the day of the first game.
"Are you ready?" asked Coach.
"Remember to work together."
Coach gave everybody a high-five.

Both teams played well.
The game was almost over.
Each team had three goals.
Adam wanted his new team to win.

First, Chuck passed the ball to Adam.
Next, Adam passed it to Lara.
Then she scored a goal.
The game was over. They won!

goal

"Good job!" said Coach.
"You played together as a team."
Adam was happy to be on the team.
He was happy to make new friends.